AF673958

COVER PAINTING

ROSHNI SHAJIL

Roshni Shajil, daughter of Shajil Anthru and Mini Shajil, Trivandrum started using colors and shades from her little age. Inspired by the litterateurs and artists in her home, Late K M Anthru (her grandfather), Shajil and Mini, she found her space in painting.

Starting from July 2017, when she was 4 years old, and continuing to design at least a cover page annually for her father. Consecutive ninth painting for book cover for father's book "Church Bells" by Roshni Shajil is one of uniqueness of this book.

Roshni S. is appreciated by India Book of Records for designing the cover page of various books. She designed the cover page of five books for her father Shajil Anthru namely 'Swapnagalile Pakshi', 'Over a Cup of Tea', 'Ey...Chu', 'Viswasahithyathile Ettavum Cheriya Kadha' and 'Janus and Other Poems', at the age of 8 years and 7 months, as confirmed on May 7, 2021.

Church Bells

Shajil Anthru

All Rights Reserved

Church Bells
Poetry Collection
2024 authored by Shajil Anthru
Book production and design (c) 2024
by Real Magazine Productions
Cover page painting (c) 2024 by
Roshni Shajil
Edited by
Mini Shajil

Printed in India
Copies 500

ISBN : 978-81-975300-6-7

Real Magazine Productions,
Trivandrum, Kerala, India.PIN 695011
Email:presidentrealmag@gmail.com
Website:https://realmagazinepro.com

For my dear ones
Mini, Roshni

and
to the living poetry legend Jack Foley, California the unquestioned master at poetry who was the first recipient of K M Anthru International Prize, 2021

and
to my late father K M Anthru, who is within me.

with special thanks to
to all the characters who prompted to create these poetry.

A Note by the Publisher

Real Magazine Productions, Trivandrum Kerala, is registered with Government of India under Ministry of Micro, Small and Medium Enterprises. We are into Retail sale via e- commerce, Publishing of books, brochures, leaflets and similar publications, including publishing encyclopedias, Higher education not leading to a degree or equivalent and Activities of individual writers, for all subjects including fictional writing, technical writing etc.

The poetry collection "Church Bells" by Shajil Anthru is the fourth book published by Real Magazine Productions. The poetry collection "Church Bells" by Shajil Anthru have many uniqueness in presentation.

The poetry in this book is a reflection of Late K M Anthru's last short story "Church Bells" written by his son, Shajil Anthru. The poetry can be termed to be under the genre "Reflectoem". Reflectoem is defined as the reflection of one's natural expressions of feelings and ideas, expressions which arise out of the basic thought that the human race is One and discrimination should not arise because of differences of languages, countries, race, creed color or gender. With the intense application of the heart either by use of distinctive styles and rhythms or by use of poetic writing in either verse or prose or by the use of art images, the movements of dance, the complex sounds of music–or the combination of all these things!–boundaries will wither away. The intense application of the heart by use of distinctive styles and rhythms, evident from the poetry of Shajil Anthru, gushing out from his heart as the natural expressions of feelings will make the readers identify with the emotions which is experienced by the characters.

The introduction to this poetry collection is nothing, but the story "Church Bells" written by Late K M Anthru. The foreword is a story "Mussel" of Shajil Anthru written in his younger days, which demonstrates his relation with his father. Moreover this book features the consecutive ninth painting for book cover for father's book "Church Bells" by Roshni Shajil. Starting from July 2017, when she was 4 years old, and continuing to design at least a cover page annually for her father. Above all, the book is edited by the author's wife Mini Shajil.

We are happy to present this book with all its uniqueness, rich in mystic and philosophical thoughts to the literature lovers of the world.

...GM

Church Bells
Reflections

Reflections

Church Bells

K M Anthru

Shivering and fogged spectacles made it difficult for him to understand that he is standing before an old house remnant, with broken windows near a chapel. The structure of the house is the same except the spiderwebs creating abstract transparent, hidden configurations onto the way to the house. There is no one to maintain the house, evident from the cracks on old painted walls

.

The dusk is yet to arrive. He took the lighter and the silver tipped Chancellor, the Virginia blend cigarette to keep the cold and slight anxiety he felt. The surroundings – lone and with no movement, not even of fallen leaves.

He was suddenly taken back by seeing a old man who appeared before him, not even giving a clue from where was coming. He asked the old man with curiosity:

"Do you know a teacher named Sarah who was staying near here or nearby?"

The old man looked at him with suspicion. His eyebrows was dropping on to his eyes. He added:

"She used to teach Hindi in this village."

The old man's voice was like a horse whisper:

"Where are you from?"

He felt something uneasy. He didn't tell the truth.

"I haven't been here for a long time. Sarah is my colleague. It's been many years since I saw her……I thought I will see her. Age is running fast."

The old man murmured and walked away.

" Sarah is gone. Her husband killed her. Don't be here. Her ghost roams here. No one comes here because they are afraid of her. A deadly revengeful ghost"

The old man diffused in the mist. He stood alone there. He looked around. Now he felt his fearful - throbbing heart.

Suddenly church bells rang. Many bells together. He looked around. Snow began to shower. He ran to a safer place and reached the old mango grove. Only one mango tree was there during the youthful moments of Sarah and him.

A sweet voice.! Is it a revelation in Sarah's voice?

"I knew you would come. I'm glad you came. I died because of you. He trampled me to death because I remembered you and never succumbed to his demand to dump you"

The church bells began to ring in unison.

The celebrity "HE" sat down in despair.

K M Anthru (1937-2020)

Mussels

Shajil Anthru

The dusk came down to the sea. The shore looks deserted. Waves still rattled into the shore in the quest of finding someone. I hung around the beach; but could not finish my combing. I am combing the damp shore for mussels. Encountering one, I will pick them up and open it. The mystic formula of my dream realization is inside a mussel.

Yes! My father once told.

"When your life becomes miserable, go to the beach. There, you will find the way to realize your dreams. It is in a mussel. "

That is why I have been here for the last few days picking and exploring each mussel I step on. I can read others- known and unknown, friends and foes, calling me crazy.

Dear readers, had you ever noticed that the sea never stopped his search for his destiny? So why should I stop?

Occasionally I chat with the waves-

"Waves... Did you ever tugged my mussel into the sea and hid it in your bosom?"

A burst of laughter would be the answer. Waves with love and empathy will come rolling towards my feet and will caress me.

Days, months, and years passed.
Only the sea and me!

Occasionally, the shower and the hurricane will shatter the shore. The blazing sun torched the sand granules. Yet neither of us stopped our probe. I stood by the sea.

Day and night;
In pain and bliss;
We are together.

Currently, no one focuses on me. Why should everyone focus on the madman? I have seen people who seasonally love and hate the sea and shore. Still, the sea sustained.

And.... One day ... it was a holiday. Holidays are a celebration, are they not? And all celebrations troop up to a place.

A girl came to the beach along with a crowd. Astonishingly, she was the lone person to sympathize with me when her mates ignored and pestered me. I heard her voice echoing from my back.

"What are you searching for?"

During the yester years, no one other than the sea asked me for such queries. I was amazed. I said. :

"The way to make my dream come true"

"Dream come true?"

She looked puzzled. I explained.

"It's in some mussel."

She said nothing and looked around. Her friends laughed mockingly.

Once again the blanket, dark and heavy, came and roofed the sea. As usual, I resorted to the beach sand in despair. That is when I saw the girl hiking towards me. She had a mussel in her palm.

She asked.

"Is this the mussel?"

I took it in my hand and opened the chip with incredible, indescribable pleasure.

Awesome! The picture of the girl, (but not the present one, her old age face) who gave me the chip looks at me from inside.

"*Yes!*"

I uttered.

When I raised my eyes, I could not see her in front of me. I looked around.

I saw her walking above the waves of the sea in harmony to its ups and down.

This story is written long back in 1980's, perhaps stories of my first phase of creative writing. At that time, I did not know, how I wrote this story or what made me write this story. Years later, now, I understand why I wrote this. - Shajil Anthru

Zebra line

You said
life is like a zebra line
it has both black and white
receive it with open hand
and smile.
you get the smile in return. '
and if you have a zebra line,
in your life
you can sail the life with ease.

Existence

Most of the times
Your existence ceases
On your demise.

But for the wretched
Their existence concludes
Halfway through their life.

Hatred are those men
Who lost their existence halfway;
And bad omen they are
for man
and humanity.

King Liar

I am the King Liar-
Who hide all *"significant"*
In my HEART.

But I do never worship
Darkness, witch craft and necromancy.

But worship
The light from your heart;
Emanating rarely
When you open its window,
Once a while
And closes suddenly,
On seeing my eyes
Stuck on it.

Yes!
I am the King Liar-
Who hide all *"significant"*
In my HEART

3, OCTOBER

October, dated 3
On calendar.
Forty five minutes passed eight
On clock.
My phone rang
To apprise me the worst.

I dashed to my sister's house
I saw my father there.
Angry, scolding – all
Not able to link his wrist watch . . .
Not able to walk . . .
I helped him sit on his chair.
While I saw the slippery
Washed off steps-
Brick particles at the edge.

No time to waste-
I rushed back to take the car
To whisk him for critical care.
There was a doctor in his home
Nothing did he do for my dad
Though he noticed the bad omen
of the blood surge in veins.

And from comatose state
My dad stripped "them" all;
to type me a helpless son
a stranded son
with all my beliefs
I acquired
during my fifty years
becoming a Capsized boat.

Delusion

I had a delusion
that you all love me.

I had a thought -
My deeds were for your "good."
I had a belief
You will never
Let me down.

But,
I understood
The very reason
I lived
and toiled -
It was in vain.

Once I moved into bed -
all started hurling stones.
I could hear a loud giggle -
See wolves and hunters -
Around me

Yes ! I had a delusion.

Exile

Alone
I go to Exile.
May be you will
Loath me -
Telling
I am leaving you.

Nay! It is not;
I want to clasp you
To my heart;
But I realize -
to clench strong
I should not be here.

Alone
I go to Exile.

Bouquet

You gifted a bouquet
and whispered -
"I love you
Love you
Can you smell my love?"

Tranquilized by the fragrance,
I reacted;
Yes, Yes, Yes !

A night after a slumber
Full of dreams,
characters- you and I;
I raised up the bouquet
Oh ! The fragrance is no more…
Its barb pierced my fingers
Red blood oozed out

And I realized;
It is not from my fingers
But from my heart.

Blossom

Flowers bloom to wither;
But you do not allow them.
Instead, you pluck them
to place on your hair.
You say it is *beauty.*

Rain downpour to quench;
But you do not allow them.
Instead, you take shelter
of overcoat or umbrella.
You say it is *safety.*

Sun burn to vitaminize;
But you do not allow him.
Instead, you stay indoors
or in air-conditioned rooms.
You say it is *tiresome.*

I came near you with love;
But you closed the doors.
Windows too
and you say it is *unfair.*
It is against GOD.

But you forgot;
Flowers, Rain, Sun and Me
are sent to you by
GOD.

Righteous

When a game is over
Another starts
When the rain stops showering
Sunlight descends to earth

When you try to provoke with
"God Himself Could Not Sink This Ship"
The iceberg comes.

When you alone are righteous
He will establish his covenant with you.

"Go into the ark
Where you will be safe
Where you will reemerge
For others to laud
You alone are righteous.
You alone are righteous"

Impeccable

Dare me NOT
Challenge me NOT
Frighten me NOT
I am impeccable
To capsize
And to exalt.

Rhythm

The rhythm of my life
is its uncertainty
the music
is its resistance to predictability
the anguish - its throb
the arrogance - its heart

Love is a cord

Love is a cord
Between the two hearts.
One could feel the heart raging
When a woe stopover other.

When you are in love
Hearts are truly exchanged.
To break a person in love
Just lie; (Remember
Not telling truth
Or half telling truth
For whatsoever reason
It is a lie.)

Yes!
When you are in love
You are not for you
You are for the other.

Magic

What magic do you have?
A touch, gesture of love
A feeling of oneness
The tide of possessiveness
How did it transform my heart?
Turbulent streamlining fast
Thought to proclaim
The heaven is here
Love for life deepens
Love to feel your radiance
Love to hold you tight
Against my heart and soul
What magic do you have?

Smell of death

I smell death
Is it my own death?
Or
Is it the death of my hope?
Or
Is it the death of my belief?
Even if it is hope and belief
It is my death
Yes!
I smell my own death.

Church bells

Church bells rang;
"..." kneeled before
the mediator of GOD
in quest of "something".
But "..." heard the mediator
- who stood calm and steady
whispering...
"An aching heart is here,
a life devoted to you
Had you seen?"

The mediator recalled!
Once she came here with a prayer,
and the mediator pronounced.
"HE is the answer to you
to guide and to be with you
instead of my 'lord'.
Church bells rang.

He lives in darkness to give you light,
He lives in pain to ensure flawless life for you.
Still! My Lord's gift is abandoned"
Church bells rang
For He is here, now
"..." kneeled before
the mediator of GOD
seeking "something".

But no one heard the mediator
- who stood calm and steady whisper....
"These church bells will ring
for him next time"

you will discover

you will discover me
when you reach the '83'
you will unearth me
when you come out
from the loop < 83
you will grasp me
when you face the trauma
of implicit desertion.

now
I can only weep
hide myself in tears!

I am certain –
you will see me
when I am shown the way
to darkness, void and emptiness.
My love will still linger
alike my ache
tears will never vaporize
and you will feel the cold
on every footstep of yours.

Love

Every genuine heart
Have a dump yard
Where others shower respect
Without knowing,
It is a place for love.

Every genuine heart
Have a strong string
Which is tied to their "love"
Their heart beats paces
With the love modulation.

But the "love" never realize.

Me and the angel

I:
"I am always with you; thinking you
Hoping you will find a way out for me
I pray always;
Act for me; Talk for me;
For I am ignorant"

The angel told:
"If the light is not visible to your eyes
If the love is not reaching your heart
If you are again feeling alone at depth
I will come to carry you to Lord
For Lord is good
His love is eternal."

Stride

We went for a stride -
You faltered upon a stone;
I warned:
"The way is full of granules -
Big and small"

You retorted:
"I am not a toddler
Learning to walk.
I know my way
I know where to step.
Now
I wavered upon a boulder;
No one could grasp me.
I trundled down to the valley,
Full of pain and darkness

On the banks of a brook

On the banks of a brook,
we heard the chirping of night birds....
we slept with the night sky
When the morning dawned,
there were
no night birds,
no night sky,
the sun smiling brightly;

how quickly did the darkness,
unfriend to vanish
embracing the scorching sun?

Swamp

Alone, with tears
a broken heart
I slid and fell deep
down the swamp.

Alone, with tears
a broken heart
I slid and fell deep
down the swamp.
Memories of smile
Vanishing beyond the view
silver bowl of desire and love
Cracked before it hit the floor

Alone, with tears
a broken heart
I slid and fell deep
down the swamp.

With a heavy left chest
in quest of a relief
Tears fill fast the swamp
Now It's only a matter of time

Alone, with tears
a broken heart
I slid and fell deep
down the swamp.

I am broken

I am broken, So
Come, Dance with me..
I am shaken, So
Come, wine with me…

Hold me with one hand
Across my belly
Hold my other hand, To
Raise up to hold the globe

Broken hearts,
Shaken hearts,
Dancing hearts
Quake the earth

...you can then hear a murmur
…Murmur of love!
...Murmur of my heart!

Pain

I feel a pain
in my heart
The blood in me is now turbulent
rushing out through the mouth and nose
as if seeking someone
Where are you
My dear
eyes become blurred
mind upset
longing for you
for you alone
break the chains
and come to hold my live
else it may scatter

flying down

Sadness creeps
Soak in heaviness

Yes
I feel drowning up
and flying down

"If he does not wake up tomorrow"

I hear a whisper
A call to far-away
from alien's land.
I hear a caution
A possible change
kindness to malice.
I can perceive the spells
Revolt to tempers
Foresee the gory floods
Tsunamic waves
Landslides in heart
Mislaid, deceased, handicapped love
Trapped in
Hurricane
Downpour
To unroot
Me and my love
-wash off to
A NO MAN LAND

Defeat

Even the five planets
Aligned near the moon
For feast my eyes
For a rarest cosmic event
In the western horizon post sunset.

But not even for five minutes
You arrived near me
For soothe my woes
Not for any marvelous event
Nay, for a caring stroke.

Signs

Looking for a signboard
I pace through the road
With ache in my heart
And hope full ....But

Wise Lord !

Like a riddle 'Mother'

Only when some ties become wobbly

'Mother cries for her son!

Disarrayed youth sealed

An ocean of love

To reach son!

Willful (?) to throw the rest of life to sea

A younger sister to own her brother

Sighs without knowing the meaning of life!

If the lost son remained in the dark,

Unknown–orphan

Hubbub would haven't risen

New squealers

Deserts the unknowable sage

Like a riddle "unknown sage"

Into a cave - cave of darkness

Fall

I am the floret
Which bloom during
The spring.

And I will wither away
Before the fall;
And the sizzling heat.

During the spring,
While the zephyr
Shriek pass me;

Not a mooring
For my words and heart
I find.

Yes!
I am the floret
-A Laughing stock

Navigation

Not even a perfect cup of coffee,
Nor a sunset stride.
in this mundane sphere
jostling to deplete all the vigor;

topsy-turvy, distressed and muddled
almost lost
old sores bursting again.

Where is the medicine?
of love and care?
the elixir of relation?

The intimacy desiccated
and the ocean floor is visible.

Though bold and open heart
Confused! how to navigate?

Ghost

I am a ghost
Who deceased because of unreached love.
I am at this grave
Amidst a lush meadow cemetery.

If you want to feel me
And to convince yourself
That I died due to unreached love
Just pluck and toss a handful of grass

You will feel my hands around you
Distinct sensation of my arms
Fantastic tactile feel, warm and calm
A feel never felt.

But you will repent
For not having eyes
While I was alive
And stalling the flow of love.

I am not a 'Cheat'

I am not a cheat;
I have love for everything;
I am a Man keen
to keep my words.

I am not a pervert;
I respect all–a human
with no discrimination;
worried of other's woes.

I am not a sadist
Nor a Narcissist/dramatist/A liar.
but fair to all
I am a human.

So, I am punished:
Punished and thrown out
Of this world;
'Never love will reach you"
……. Devil and God unanimously professed.

Athens is burning

Athens is burning   my heart too
wildfire is raging,
firefighters,
water-bombing aircrafts
    Nothing stops the fire.

Gales; altering course   inside my heart too
surge the ferocious blaze
ash rain downfalls
and homes collapse
    humans, animals all alike.

evacuations from home,   isolation for me
hometown and globe
'We couldn't breathe'
yells the Greeks.
    panic seeks for aid.

Where is Itus – the God?
Protector of Apollo
Upon his compulsion
ate the ambrosia
    to become a GOD

Where are the Xenios and Kurios
You had to protect the innocent
from those whom would do harm.

Where are you?

Itus....
    We, the innocents are burnt.   buried

a tribute to Sitaram Yechury from a Man from void

Comrade

Comrade
is no more feeling
the sensation
And you called it death!

But dear comrades,
Marx once said;
and you often forget
alive in the avaricious era.

"-Those men are the supreme;
dignified human toiling hard
for the common GOOD
-Happiest are those humans;
Sweated profusely making
a content set of HUMANS."

Comrade
is no more feeling
the sensation.
But we can see him ennobled
We can see his happiness!

Smile of Marx

A hard rock on my trunk...Aah!
Remnant of Landslide;
Granules of Woe Accrued;
Mercilessly upon my life.

For my yearned last drop,
flood override on me.
Corpse of man, dog and hen
along the same offshoot.

Marx appeared with a smile:
A while he took to speak:
A commune has come
where all are equal ! ! !

No one is more equal !
No one speak hatred !
No religion, caste or creed !
Economic diversity, race !

State withered away !
The law of Nature Thrive !
Where Man fail, Nature win !

Darkness grew before me
and I hear no voice.
I remember nothing,
except the smile
-Smile of Marx.

Bubble gum

banned not are the bubble gums
multicolor, various designs, shapes;
they come covered with attractive covers-
aesthetic and tempting;
ingredients, percentage, written
on wrapper fully untrue.

Chew, chew, chew...
you get intoxicated
voluptuous and sadist.
Laugh
cry
shout
like drugged.

vocal cord can vomit
defame and demean
sweetness
bitterness
saltness
spicy
...passes through your tongue
In the arteries of the brain
to drive you crazy.

But...
The truth alone will not suffice.

The truth is now in ashes;
No chance, not even for a postmortem;
Now the seekers of truth
are bubble gum chewers.

They create "truths".
"victims" are in the making.
To hide the bare truths
They act furious.
When bare truths stay
ashes on the pyre,
The truths framed by
coated gum chewers will reign.
But...
the day is near
For ashes from the pyre,
to raise and form the "E.T."

true story of lady-dark and short

Professor

I know a professor – a lady
She is the best in pampering girls
One day, in her class, a married student
Upset over her new wed boy
Cried in class in front of sadistic friends
To add a bit of pain, they too affronted.

Lady Professor, happy she was to get a prey
Told her to send a voice message of suicide
Accusing her friends so that they study a lesson.
WhatsApp message – it went with a lightning speed
Lady Professor advised the other students to complain
That they are threatened and the new wed girl is mad.

Lady Professor – pious and ideal – acted
Helpless; pathetic about the new gen girls
Asked one by one to come for counselling
At evening with a sip of coffee to resolve
One by one – girls went – but – with rape drugs
They were put for sale – one month salary
For the professor for two-hour rehab.

When you scorch the daily!

You will pronounce
yourself as GOD;
You will scorch the daily
which embossed my words;

You will alter the gist
of my words;
You,
[Not even having the valor
to kick a grit]
will goad to slay
words-
letters-
Sentences-
Thoughts-

And
those who love the words;
the sound of
letters,
words,
views,
even silences -
will make you tremble.

The heights of your cowardice
will lure you to send "them"
to prey upon me.

Yes!
in the same daily-
my words embossed;

the same daily
you scorched in mid-day,
You will highlight my heroic tales,
dribble tears and moan.

As if you are a victor
you will look the mirror;
But you will scream;
Flee
barefooted
streak
on to the street...

expose the nudity
of both physique and soul.

It was the day of Mussolini

a dagger between his teeth
a bomb in his hand
cynicism in his heart
arrogance in his eyes

morals, vaunt he sang
avowed, unassailable
democracy, sweetened theory
but truth, it is a bitter!

you love the melody of Sparrows
but it is not good that eagles fall
glide along the vultures to hunt
and strangle the sparrow neck

I am always right,
wrong are those disagree
crowds, whoever- avoid
and seat high from them

paparazzi can chant
I am toiling hard for them.

(Laughter)

without pagers
with words...
he
scattered the heart
of his folks.

Day and Night

The night will be black
The moon will bleach
The day will be white
And the sun will blacken

You had a word
You had a voice
We banked on you
Your words and your voice.

What did you articulate?
"See the realm
With the pair of glasses"-
You gifted one
"No hue or tint
Colorless neutral glasses.
You see what truly is."

But
On the day of eclipse
We found
Your glass is dyed
Our life is stained
With fake views and thoughts

The cat, rat and the King

There was a cat
Cat was like a “rat”
Rat sat on the lap
- lap of the King.
Cat, rat and King
scared by sounds -
send their militias
to kill even the hums.

And they -
Sat on the couch
giggled to see
man on the mat
and the mat was pulled
sandy grains on the man
the fountain of echoes.

it is funny...
proclaimed their massive shaky
bellies.

But...
they were sliding down on their bellies.
- The cat, rat and the King.

Why I am a Victim?

Adam and Eve
Walked through the Eden Garden
Looking here and there
Hands tied each other
Shoulder near to shoulder
Sometimes drawing closer
Kissing, laughing and in muse
Oh! Get me that apple dear
Eve craved for the red one
Adam jumped up. NO!
The height is too much
Soon he found a stick
The first tool he took
Apple came down
And now with the same stick
Devil shown to Adam,
Conscience strike on my back

When I stand

Alone

Alone

Alone

Have you ever?

Had you ever noticed?
    there is a time
    there is a place
    there is a moment
    overturning your life.

Had you ever perceived?
    there are beliefs
    there are contradicting beliefs
    some stay giving you a way
    some stay against your way.

Had you ever recognized?
    there is reality
    there is virtuality

Sometimes reality is
    better(bitter) than virtuality

Sometimes virtuality is
    better(bitter) than reality.

Had you ever wrestled with?
    there is sickness
    there is stickiness
        one with body
        the other with soul.

Had you ever seen?
    sometimes intuition guides you
    sometimes facts guide you

Both direct you to (mis) growth
If you never have a dream space.

Have you ever realized?
    silent universe, its landscapes- virgin;
    the dreamscapes of inner soul
            both are life changing.

Have you ever noticed?
     you have to
        embrace the…
        inspire ...
        evolve into…

But who and what-
Do you possess an answer?

Life – a fishbone poetry

between warmth and loathing
between distant and near
between stormy and calm
between mirth and misery
between bliss and anguish
we cruise our life
between passion and weary
between devotion and ennui
between dreams and truth
between reception and rejection
between humane and decadent

For you- a fishbone poetry

My eyes
My ears
My hand
My words
My heart
My thoughts
My life
For you, - For you -For you - For you - For you - For you
To Soulify
To Care
With Love
To hear
To hold
To whisper
My dear

With and within me

I won't say
I am the GOD
Instead, I will say
GOD is within me
Alongside the devil.

I won't say
I am the SUN
Instead, I will say
SUN is with me
Alike the moon.

Flower

Through the window pane
I saw your love -
Like a sprout
Zealous for blossoming
to emanate the fragrance
to soothe my eyes with colors
and to feel your softness.

Yes!
I opened the window pane -
and suddenly I discovered;
It was just a painting of an artist -
Vivid and dazzling,
Upon the glass of the pane.

Sea

Have to cry;
Burst into tears;
Hide my tears against her bosom.

The rhythm in her bosom is
enough to resolve the grief.
She's enough!

She said:
I am the sea-
The sea that accepts any sorrow!

Ready
to accept everything
Good or bad.

Voyagers sail upon my waves
Inducing pain
through their oars.

They never realize...
How much pain
I feel on every plunge,
Along with their song.

Still I wait and wait;
Seek and seek ;
My love to come
yo rest my head on her lap.

That's why
I jumped into the sea!

She is no more

She is no more
She is no more
She is no more
by word of mouth
it rolled to me.

I saw her
stiff body
wrapped in white
after the last bath
with sandalwood paste
flowers and basil petals
around and upon her.

And she rests
in the glass casket
silent and calm.

Chants and hymns
Prayers and praise
Yell, scream-all
I heard.

Crematorium too
came towards her.
at her window side.
where her toes
often made impressions.
in the midst of the plants
she watered and cared

Church Bells

And when it was lit
with her body inside
I saw the white fumes
dancing up with
tune of nature
tune of unknown

An aura of
helplessness
void
a question
blurred the view.

From where she came
To where she went,
Darkness to darkness?

I don't know.
I knew only
I never saw her live.
And
She is no more.

Kite

sounds, clatters,
hush,
now
in Mute mode

light, colors
colorlessness
also
in dark mode

darkness,
buoyancy
all
active now

the one who guides
the thump of the heart
of kite
didn't recall

If you give up
It just breaks
my ...
life for ever.

'Kings and Queens'

A sharp knife groove deep cut
into the mutton piece – a leg;
the marinade ingredients brushed
and spiced up the dead lamb.

Heated lifeless limb bone's
marrow gets stewed and soft.
and it boards the ivory table
where the Kings and queens dine.

Kings drink and chew the flesh;
Queens suck the limb bone in secret,
for they knew the marrows are rich
full of collagen, glucosamine.

Morning next, at the yard
dogs fight for the bones.
Nay, they are hollow;
Nay, they are hardened.

Like my life - weird and dumped
even stray dogs don't need
And I wonder why 'Kings and Queens'
eat and dump me in the street.

Clown

I am into complete solitude and isolation
which no one can comprehend.
Like a clown,
I perform with my heart
plucked out from my trunk- trying to confirm you-this is my heart, this is my heart-
but all my yell is rumbling back to me

I am now in total desolation.
I can hear the murmur of the gush.
-the sound of the gale
They are nearing me

Song

I hear
The song of a heart
Soaked and about to burst
But I did not see him/her
Which realm the core
But the song is real
I hear.

Yes!
It is from me!
It is in me!
It is for me!
It is me!

Cassandra

Cassandra...
You are a woman;
I am a Man.
But we are ONE
From two era.

you knew what was up,
but no one knows what was up with you
As with me.

All your thoughts were pickled
as ramblings of a maniac,
poor Cassandra
though predictions
accurate, she made
but not a prophetess
she owned.
the fall of Troy
the death of Agamemnon,
She warned
then went unheeded.

No one realized
There is a 'give and receive'
in all relationships.
But
Alas!
You,
Cassandra is always fated
For a one-way bond
As with me

Used paper cups
"Not fit for reuse"

"As above, so below; As below, so above.

"As above, so below;
As below, so above.
As within, so without;
As without, so within."
Our life rolls onward
The turns of vagueness.
I loved a woman
I showed her how
I am devoted
Why my heart beats.

Impossible to love like this
She said in disbelief.
I wished to show
her my heart rhythm
When she is not with me.

But still:
"As above, so below;
As below, so above.
As within, so without;
As without, so within."

Gentle man

I am not a Gentle man
Since I am not a man of noble birth
Nor a man who belongs to the landed gentry
Or have any rank with chivalrous qualities

I am not a Gentle man
Since I am not a man with conformity
To high standard of propriety
Or a man of independent means

I am not a Gentle man
Since I do not engage
In any menial occupation
Or anything for "gain"

I am not a Gentle man
Since I am not free from
Harshness and Sternness;
Passiveness and Softness.

I am not a Gentle man
Since I am never honored /distinguished
I never raised glasses with vine
To firm the harmony.

I am not a Gentle man
Since no one ever found
Any love in my heart
Actions, words and life

Lip and Cup

Lip and cup
Both I like
Lip to kiss
Cup full of tea
But I lost both
Between cup and lip

Flying high

I through the peeping hole
Watched the bird flying.

I fashioned flying in dreams
Feathers waxed to my body.

As I flew high and high
All below clapped and rejoiced.

But by the torching heat
The wax melt and the feathers
Floated away to bring me down
To sink in sea; the turbulent sea.

Exile

Not even a hug you gave
Not even a word you told
Sixty- Four years of exile
What for the three words
Now you ask from me?

Do you know how am I now?
Lost in despair and hidden
Sadness creeps every moment…
Every second of my life...
I am cheated- betrayed!

I used to fight with my love
But now I lost the right to fight
I lost the right to love
I feel mediocre
Landed in a no love region

He is no more

He is no more
He is not dead
But he is not seen
He had disappeared

Where did he go?
Sky?
Earth?
Beneath?

Who had engulfed him?
Fire?
Sand?
Vultures?

He is no more
He is not dead
But he is not seen
He had disappeared

Let me give an ad -
Anyone met
true Love?
anywhere?
anytime?

For Peace, I...

Transients of ache
blood sprouts
recap the spout
-spring from the heaven
upheaval for peace.

tissues - all soggy
hired out for the marsh
to bestow peace upon you.
Never a sacrifice,
And not with tears.

Nay! the goodness is
Not
numb
speechless
in dark
or clumsy.

Still, I am.

Pillow

two in laws I have, my son-
I chose one
a doctor for my daughter;
other you chose, an engineer.

Old age and stroke
On bed I got stuck.
Ache and anguish,
Sometimes, I growl -screech;

inept to spot
the spring of hurt.

One night, the doctor- in law
Strode down to my cot;
commanded to be mum
my pain broke his sleep.

I snapped back by howling,
And do you know, my son?

He pulled off my pillow;
And when I tried to rise
he knocked hard my face
and forced the head hit the wall.

oh! what a pain it was?
a darkness feast, has
my breath stuck?
No! I have little forte
To drive the darkness away;
I saw- he trying to stifle me
With the pillow; with a smile
my wife and daughter there.

Church Bells

Good, that you took me here
where there is no one else
my son, in law, my wife
and my pet granddaughter.

While I sat on the settee,
suddenly slanted to on end
and about to fall- today;
and my eyes got wet,

to see my in-law pacing
with a pillow – the barrier
for my head and the wooden bar
Luckily, your chosen one is not a doctor.

Poison globules in return to chocolates

Betrayal

The little boy called my father (young in his 30's)
"chocolate uncle" - thanks for the sweet boxes.
step brother-in-law, the little boy he was
my mother's pet throughout her life-

Little boy in his middle age, sly and craving
Betrayed my father (old in 80's)
for not just 30 pieces of silver
gave sweet globules, poison immersed.

Unlawful life, the step brother-in law led
Slayed many for his gains
Relations and emotions, he never cares
And lives scot-free in this world.

Unlike others, my father
commenced his war
with life and death
from 3 October 2017.

Before the last breath
He wrote:
"Get him punished- He is a mafia: the details are here"
But the law is blind;

And the killer is in the streets
Searching for new prey.

I am hacked!

I am hacked!
Both past tense and past participle apply.
Yes! My life is hacked.

Did they think?
my deeds for the deprived
are dead branches
to chop off.

Did they think?
to terminate me by
hacking my neurons
to steal the ingenuity.

But did they overlook?
my roots to Prometheus
- Snatcher of Fire from Gods
 to gift the humanity
- creator of humankind
from clay.

Didn't they think?
 by hacking and thieving
humanity-
Like the eagle eaten liver
of Prometheus,
growing every overnight,
they will never succeed
to overturn the humanity.

Lost

How can I tell about me?
I am...Like...Lost.

Lost in the middle of the sea -
roaring waves brash upon me
captivating me
and throwing me madly.

Yes!
What can I tell about me?
I am...Like...Lost
Lost In the middle of a desert -
scorching sun beneath my legs;
wavering legs plunge in the sand;
dust storm makes my eyes blind;
and tears roll down

Yes!
Shall I tell about me?
I am...Like...Lost.
Lost In the middle of a forest -
dense forest;
wild silence and whistles.
awful hikes,
and no sun and hope.

Even the fall of a leaf
frighten me.
Yes!
I am...Like...Lost.

Ache

My heart beat just to
thrust oxygenated blood into the body.

My heart beats just to
drive hormones to the body.

My heart beats just to
receive de-oxygenated blood.

My heart beats just to
propel lungs for oxygenation

My heart beats just to
sustain my blood pressure.

Yet it gets an ache
When you fade from my vision,

Yet it gets an ache
When your words do not reach my ears,

Yet it gets an ache
When your fragrance does not reach me,

Yet it gets an ache
When your touch fails,

Yet it gets a pain
When my taste buds fails.

And I feel it is better NOT to pump
If there is no prospect of removing
the cause of the ache.

Lullaby

Sleep....
My son told
Sleep...
My son requested
Close your eyes
And say yourselves
I am going to sleep
I am going to sleep
I am going to sleep.
You will sleep.
This is my promise...

But I closed my eyes
It unwrapped my mind
It unbolted my heart
Blood rushed
But it was not blood
It was thoughts
It was not thoughts
It was you
You
You
And you
Only.

Today is my birthday

Today is my birthday...
Is it one more year
of collaboration with light?
Or another step
to experience once again, the dark?

Yes!
I remember -
Before my birth, I was here;
During my "life" I am here;
After my "death" I will be here;

Before my birth,
DARKNESS blanketed my eyes.
During my "life",
DARKNESS of in humanity frequently made me blind.
After my "death"
again, that DARKNESS will engulf me.

Did I gain one more year of experience?
Did I move one step towards my next board?

But unlike other birthdays
I feel dumped, pushed off
to a new plane where I found
the innocence of street boys.
wickedness, elite malice.
I feel all chains are broken
all boundaries for me had withered
My soul is now prepared
the "virus - tamed" too-

to start, rejoin;
traverse where I stopped.

War and Love

When the war is raging
inside my heart;
the silence becomes the shell
thrown into my bunker
of isolation and solitude.

When the gyratory globe
reminds the resolute stillness;
the silence becomes the rifle
pointed close to my heart
throbbing for you.

When love-less-ness is haunting
even at the outskirts of heart;
The silence of 'one' amidst clatter,
bombs the streamlined course
of blood and thoughts.

When the occurrence
begins to grow tall enough to remind you,
whatever you are-you are naught;
it is more than
a point-blank pistol.

Murmur of love!

I am broken, So
Come, Dance with me...
I am shaken, So
Come, wine with me…

Hold me with one hand
Across my belly
Hold my other hand, To
Raise up to hold the globe

Broken hearts,
Shaken hearts,
Dancing hearts
Quake the earth

…you can then hear a murmur
…Murmur of love!
... Murmur of my heart!

Within me; With me!

I met Carter yesterday
I saw the eagle
I met the Sudanese child
- All in my neighborhood.
I saw the murderer flee
I jumped over the corpse.
I felt the heat of brutality
- All in my neighborhood.
I heard the ache and silent starvation
I passed by the wounded - (inside and outside)
I sneaked off the Trigger-Happy Maniacs.
- All in my neighborhood.
Speaking at a defense meet
I realize. ..
- All in my neighborhood
are within me; with me!

The man behind the lens of one of the most heartbreaking photographs of the century. He photographed a Sudanese child, starved almost to death, crouching with her head buried in her tiny hands while a vulture awaits her death so that it could devour the corpse. Carter chased the vulture away after taking the shot, but couldn't do much to help the girl. This photograph, depicting the poverty, destitute and famine fetched Carter the Pulitzer prize in 1994. After suffering from depression for months, Carter finally committed suicide in 1994. He was only 33 at the time of his death.

Deadly Life

[*Lines 5 to 13 is from (The Bell Jar)* - *Sylvia Plath* (1932 – 1963)]

Oh!
My Sylvia

Your words reverberate
Loud as a silent evening;

"Death must be so beautiful.
To lie in the soft brown earth,
with the grasses waving above
one's head,
and listen to silence.
To have no yesterday,
and no tomorrow.
To forget time,
to forgive life,
to be at peace."

Life must also be beautiful
If we lie down
Much beneath the crest of the grass
And be silent.
No thoughts about the past
and future.
Forget time
Forget life
Forget peace
Forget yourselves.
Let
  drizzle
  torrent
  thunder
  breeze
  gale
  day
  night
come

You will be there
If you are beneath the grass
Like a stray
in dump yard.

Abandoned

Yes!
I am abandoned;
just left out completely
expecting of no longer usable
of no longer needed
as a paper cup.
Yes!
I am hunted
to wash off my portrait
from the canvas of life
expecting of prospective risk
from truth (may I Disclose?)

Yes!
Like Shelley
who travelled in an open boat-
with an open book
Of life.
Through the turbulent
sea and life.
Odd to the society
often dumped and thrown out.
who sank down to the sea bed,
with a copy of Keats's Lamia.
But when his rotting body
torched to ashes;
his heart resisted burning
calcified with woes and qualms;
and it remained as such.

Will my heart resist the heat?
My heart
calcified by unreached love,
hate and neglect.
Will my heart resist the heat?

The gift

Anne,
every day, everyone paints their being with watercolor
true it is, all know they will be washed off once;
when – how - by whom is a mystery-
still, many watercolor paintings are budding.

I too played with colors on a canvas
but there were no approving eyes;
And when I finished this canvas,
everyone started pelting me with pebbles.

They deem this is the full stop of my print;
But, it is not a full stop; but a semicolon.
If there still exists,
the gift once bestowed upon me by the universe.

Anne Sexton once told, ("For My Lover, Returning to his Wife")
"As for me, I am a watercolor. I wash off."
Why did she say to the reporter that she would not permit the poems to be published before her death? In October 1974, with the manuscript complete, she met with poet Maxine Kumin to revise galleys of the book, set to be published the following March. She returned home from the lunch meeting, donned her mother's old fur coat, poured her vodka, and locked her in the garage with the car running, dying of gaseous poisoning.

God believer-pretend taking off the life of his uncle - cheating his uncle's trust

A true story

He believed in his nephew
Religious and pious
He regretted, not to teach his son
Religion and rituals.

His nephew must perform his last rites
Mom told the son- it is father's wish
Son – bound to obey his "father' wish"
The day of coma was forced
He sustained with the help of oxygen.

Friends came, relatives came
All told their opinion.
He will die; he had died
One said- only his body remain.
His son waited miracle to happen
His son wanted his father back
His daughter slept well; his wife too
Only his son, daughter in law
and granddaughter awake.

His nephew came on Wednesday
Told secretly to his son in law
Don't let his son know
Friday, if buried, will go to heaven

He believed in his nephew
Religious and pious
Upon his words the son in-law came
At midnight to instruct the home nurse
'unplug the oxy machine'

His son, daughter in law awake
This son in law went back.
So was his nephew
Religious and pious.

One day later
On the same date and time
His mother said "Good bye"
He went with his mother.

But...
He regretted not,
to teach his son
Religion and rituals.
Since his son is still a human.
His son is a human.

Dedicated to the paparazzies who tainted his life

Peeping Aunt

"His" means was a camera
under a veil
with a blade
concealed on the tripod.
"He" was in the Eastman movie
"Peeping Tom" (1960)
Michael Powell as director
Mark Lewis, the character of "He".
Lewis, wary and cloistered
lives in a home alone.
films the last moments
of his seduced prey facing death
by his tripod blade.
And
laughs and walks away.

Another sixty years rolled
Now "He" is "She"

"Her" tool was her eyes
hidden thoughts
like a blade
concealed to kill.
"She" is not in the Eastman movie
but a west salt estuarian.
egotistic
Lady Lord, her conduct.
Acts, modest and reclusive
lives in a home alone.
paparazzi her known ones
what for, no one knew
And
laughs with a clap and one leg up.

It is not like a dream.

It is not like a dream.

White clouds sliding down the heaven with wings of angels swaying away the heat of sun and patting me in the breezeless vacuity bestowed upon me - steady but floating with my feet not feeling the ground.

It is not like a dream.

Elevated up to the world where angels and devils abide composed unexpectedly like a broken kite, when the hand of love which held me undid the grip and let go for a flash to gift me this desolation.

It is not like a dream.

The disposition at the imprudent moment to drop the faith bequeathed upon me - betraying the poise to march ahead in togetherness was like sneaking into the Eden to sin.

It is not like a dream.

Defenselessly seeing the unfurled tears of love, holding palm blemished by blood when the clasp was loosened, while clewing high, could just lament overwhelmingly which the thunder muted in its vociferous thud.

It is not like a dream.
The sound of slaughterer honing the vanes for my nerves resonates as the music of emptiness with the dancing cloud which offer my eyes a wooziness of unsteadiness.

It is a reality.

Resuscitation

I lost my sound...
Life cords abruptly proclaimed halt;
Larynx of life are not embraced by the breeze-
breeze of love.

It is not the soreness
-Of the past;
-Of the bad memories;
May be it is bulge of frosty tears.

It is not from outside worm;
But from inside of my heart.

Doctor...
Give me a resuscitation...
Let your lips tell me the meaning of life.

Kiss

You kiss me...
Ha! The brew of oxytocin, dopamine and serotine
with fewer Cortisol;
I go exhilarated.
Affection and fondness grow tall;
My angst drive down,
Imbedding jubilant flashes.
Ha! The blood vessels widens
Pressure - Spasms
Shrinks
No more headache but boundless care.
Kiss me ...
Dear ...
The mighty death.

no one can see

Yes
No one can see
No one can see my heart
No one can see my heart throbbing
No one can see my heart throbbing in love
No one can see my heart throbbing in love for you
No one can see my heart throbbing in love for you since I met you
No one can see my heart throbbing in love for you since I met you, but in my late evening
No one can see my heart throbbing in love for you since I met you, but in my late evening filled with blur.

The world has nothing to say

The world has nothing to tell me; except silence !

Mystic and boundless;
Though
Branches creak,
Squirrels chatter,
Leaves rustle,
Floor crick,
Boughs Crackle,
Foliage crunch,
Wind whistle,
Birds hum,
Lizards scrabble,
Buzz of insects,
Yelp of frogs,
Shriek of birds,
Scuttle of mammals,
Snuffle of boar,
Scamper of hares,
Screech of jays,
Shamble of badgers,
Loping of wolves,
Slinging of wildcats,
Scurry of squirrels,
Scuttle of rabbits,
Skitter of mice,
Lumbering if bears,
And click of bats-
Under the cover of silence,
Swollen noise in humid air
with an outer covering of silence.

The world has nothing to tell me; except silence
Silence of boundless sound –scary and varied.

Last evening in my life

I feel nervous . . .
My hands are shivering;
My legs are trembling;
My tongue is slipping;
My eyes are drooping;
My ears turned deaf.
I do not feel the earth;
I do not feel the breeze;
I do not see the sky;
I do not feel (your) love;
I do not feel the warmth.
True! It happened because
a volcano erupted inside my heart.
No one knew deep inside my heart
It was so hot.
The heart itself melted,
mixed with the love (My).
Magma raised and raised
To erupt.
No one noticed the
thin, runny gaseous magma;
Invisible to heartless eyes.
Nay! I will not throw away the tephra
just will flow slowly;
Giving time for you to escape.
It won't blast off-
It will slowly flow
from my heart
to meet
my last evening
of my life

-Good Bye

My father

Silence is his language
He who taught me to toddle
In this world
With
Smile
Words
Emotions
Closed eyes mouth half open
to oxy mask.
He lay steady
The difficult take of breath
Ups and downs of chest '
Reflecting the ups and down of his life.
Oh! It is pacing down
Pacing down – the O 2 saturation
Heart rate too.
Father…
Your last words were
Shajil, are you here?
Yes ! Father
I am here
Can you feel my massage on chest
Can you feel my palm on head
Can you hear me
Can you open your eyes-for a moment, please?
Father…
Slow down not
For I can't stand…

Father ....
He who taught me to toddle
In this world
With
Smile
Words
Emotions
Succumbed

On 19 December 2020, 225 AM IST
Making me lone
Embedding with the treasures of secrets.

Crown

Let this world sleep, sleep and sleep . . .
Let the stars twinkle, twinkle and twinkle . . .
For I am here -
a charred star
alone, alone and thrown away
waiting for a 'thorn' crown

Church Bells

Shajil Anthru

Cover Design
Roshni Shajil

Shajil Anthru
Multilingual litterateur who wrote the world's shortest story; Founder of Zeroism and Fish bone poetry. Author, Editor, Poet and Philosopher

Include

Shajil Anthru's eighty three poetry(K M Anthru passed away at the age of 83) along with Late K M Anthru's last story "Church Bells " as introduction, Shajil Anthru's Story "Mussels" as Foreword, and Consecutive ninth painting for father's book cover ["Church Bells"] by Roshni Shajil. Starting from July 2017, when Roshni was 4 years old, she continue to paint and design at least one cover page annually for her father.

"Elegant and naive works", this is how Paul Klee defined his childish drawings. Elegant and naive, it seems to me, this artistic work of Roshni, especially for her ability to look at the world in an innocent way, capable of pointing directly to its symbolic representation. A world of colors, hers, where there is no trace of the "ugliness" that dominates our time.

Giacomo Cuttone, Artist from Italy about Roshni's Cover painting

ISBN : 978-81-975300-6-7

www.ingramcontent.com/pod-product-compliance
Lightning Source LLC
Chambersburg PA
CBHW022200160726
48282CB00024B/261
* 9 7 8 8 1 9 7 5 3 0 0 6 7 *